My Puddles

Thai Peck

BALBOA.
PRESS
A DIVISION OF HAY HOUSE

Balboa Press books may be ordered through booksellers or by contacting:

Balboa Press
A Division of Hay House
1663 Liberty Drive
Bloomington, IN 47403
www.balboapress.com.au
1 (877) 407-4847

Print information available on the last page.

ISBN: 978-1-5043-1277-6 (sc)
ISBN: 978-1-5043-1278-3 (e)

Balboa Press rev. date: 03/27/2018

This memoir was written with love and gratitude
to the memory of my late husband Brian Peck

Contents

Introduction

"*What an exciting, creative and challenging tale Thai have written, richly and artistically well positioned with images, verses and poems. The story from snippets of her life as well as her husband's is insightful, also portraying history of the World in their lifetime. It is a true treasure for her children and grandchildren to understand her journey.*" Sandy Wollenberg

"*...It's also a story of great love; great dreams, of childhood pain, sadness, and grief and also with immense joy are part of Thai's life, which she has so eloquently expressed in this unique tale. Flowing, self-assured, beautifully written and wonderfully constructed.*" Barbara Boetker

"*Thai's memoir is an intriguing narrative in its sensitivity of her writing, we enjoyed learning how she overcame obstacles to manage her life in the world.*" Di and Tony Short

"*It is refreshing to read raw, bold and heartfelt writing providing an historical snapshot about enduring love. You become absorbed in Thai's journey of the emotional rollercoaster that is life.*" Dan-Thy Nguyen.

I would like to dedicate this story to my daughter who has been there for me from the beginning. My writing would have not been realised without her encouragement and support. I know wherever he is Brian is smiling on us.

Preface

"...This feeling is like a wonderful sting. I want this feeling to hold me captive. I wouldn't give this up, not even for all seasons to be spring..."
David P. Leverett

He was back! Back from nowhere with no explanation. Though puzzled I was not shocked nor angry but somewhat motionless. A little crossed perhaps at his reappearance after almost two years.

My heart softened as I looked at his handsome face beaming with the familiar cheerful smile, his eyes twinkled with irrepressible mischief yet not a word uttered. I could not help but forgiving him and his long absence. *"Where did he go?"*

We were at a concert where there were so many people attending; the theatre was full. Although I was still uneasy about his disappearance, it was not a place for any reproachful discussion. As we were making our way toward our seats I was pleased noticing the seats seemed to be a lot roomier and more comfortable than I remembered, they were more like Business Class seats on a Qantas flight, I made a comment about it. He did not seem to hear nor care, he made no reply but his eyes continued to study my face as though he was looking for some sort of reaction from me as in the past, when he knew he was in my "bad book".

The lights dimmed as the conductor tapped his baton, the orchestra started softly with the violins, then the music slowly expanded into the sound of the violas followed by the cellos and finally filled the large hall, as the wind instruments joined in full force. I felt a gentle touch on my left hand, it was raised and his soft lips planted a long, tender kiss on it.

In the past I would have turned toward him and in the half darkness, our eyes would have found each others, I would have responded with a gentle squeeze on the hand and we would have mimed our lips to: "*I love you*".

I made no attempt to even cast a glance in his direction, nor searching for his eyes, I stayed motionless, a confused thought ran through my head and I felt almost numbed when my left hand returned to its position on my lap... The music gradually reaching a crescendo... "*Why is he back?*"

At home we got ready for bed. Unlike in the past, he did not insist lying on his preferred side of the bed. In his absence

I have moved the bed around and have been lying on his favourite side, my head on his pillow. To my surprise he was quite happy and cheerfully walking around to the other side of the bed. Once in bed he seemed to settle himself more in the middle of the bed, which left me with not much room. And unlike in the past, I would have muttered cheekily: "Move over buster!" Instead, I seemed to accept without any fuss and settled myself as comfortably as I could.

The bedside lamp was turned off and in darkness I could feel his hand reaching for mine, a feeling of great comfort - the familiar sensation of his skin touching mine; the movements of our wrists, our hands, our fingers caressing each other one by one, greeting with longing and loving. I could feel this strange familiar tight stretched skin in the palm of his hand... I closed my eyes breathing in the realisation of how much I have missed this beautiful and magical feeling that slowly penetrating through every vein of my body.

It was so real, so familiar but at the same time, how strange! I heard myself whispering softly in darkness: *"Why are you back?"*

In a perfect silence I heard no reply and when I opened my eyes, I was again, all alone!

My eyes were dry and the music was still playing... It was but a dream.

1

Puddle

As a child I used to think if I stepped into a puddle, I would be in another world, and a dreamer I still am. Fairy tales were never allowed in the household as they represented something sinful. I was double sin when I somehow possessed a couple of them, which hidden under my bed, I thought were safe and that no one would ever be able to find. How wrong was I. My favourite story was "Beauty and the Beast" and the part when Belle was given a ring that enabled her to see her home village. For me, I tried to imagine that I could see into another world far, far away from my parents' home.

Staring into the puddle I could see the sky that looked totally different from the sky above me. Then behind me came a voice that belonged to an adult:

"Don't walk in the puddle!"

As an adult I sometime heard myself say the same thing to my children and grandchildren - I thought to myself: "How boring you are!"

Saigon 1952

Saigon in the rain

Growing up in South-east Asia, I had plenty of puddles to walk in. In the rain muddy puddles appeared practically everywhere, and countless times, to the annoyances of the adults, I stepped in them. Time after time I was disappointed – I had gone nowhere only to be told off, severely at times or punished for my deliberate actions. Then one day the world came to me! Though I still had to grow up many more years before I could get away from the environment I was born into, I never felt a sense of belonging, however strange that may seem. Saigon then was not an easy time or place to grow up in, but the image of the puddle kept me struggling and surviving through many difficult years of my transformation from childhood to young adult and to the age twenty-one.

Recalling my growing up years in my parents' domain would be too painful, and it would be impossible for me to find words to write them down. The one thing I most remembered as a young child was that – all I craved for was to love and be loved. The image that seemed to have stayed in my soul and my mind almost forever: "A little girl tiptoeing into her parents' bedroom, when there was no one about. On the left side of the bed – a soft fluffy white pillow where her mother laid her head nightly. The little girl buried her face into it, with her eyes closed she slowly inhaled the lovely fragrance of a particular perfume..." That's how I felt a mother's love. I grew up content with that "love" whenever I needed some comfort.

The only "adult" I would remember with a certain affection was my maternal grandmother. It was for only one short week of my entire life that I had the chance to be with her. I think I was only a small child of 9 or 10 years old I don't remember why I was allowed to do so, in a way that was quite unusual as I never really knew or had much contact with my grandmother. The precious memory of that special week has stayed in my mind so vividly ever since.

Through a young child's eyes, my grandmother looked ancient, she never worn any perfume and her skin was lined with deep wrinkles. Her teeth were all black from chewing areca nuts wrapped in lime betel leaves; my grandmother must have been chewing them for many, many years because her teeth were looked like they had been washed in black ink. Her smile would send many little kids running away crying yet I was fascinated with the blackness, I wondered how she kept them so black and so shiny??? I have learned quite a lot in that week being away from my parents' house. That was to be my destiny: "The further I got away from my parents, the more I'd get to learn in life."

My grandmother was poor she lived in a small village by the river. A muddy road lead the way to her house, which was made out of straw and bamboo and worn wooden floorboards. It had just 2 rooms; the front one was larger with a couple of old easy chairs and a wooden "coffee" table at the front. Toward the back wall you could see a curtain divided the room, behind the curtain was a "double bed" divan and a chest-of-drawers; that was the bedroom! The other room was the kitchen with a brick range where one did all the cooking over a couple of clay pots. A huge water storage container sat by the cooking range; this fresh water was collected from the rain and a nearby well where all the villagers gathered daily for "networking", mostly women and girls. I remembered hearing lots of laughter and gossips. I had no idea what they were talking about, but I enjoyed being there just to see how happy the women were.

I slept in the kitchen on a little canvas bed when my grandmother's boyfriend came to visit, other nights I could sleep on the big divan with my grandmother and that was nice. Now, the outhouse was way, way back behind the house, you had to walk on the wooden plank out over the river to get there, you can imagine the rest.

I never knew my grandmother's name; I only called her "grandma". She never formally introduced me to her boyfriend so I never knew his name or what to call him either. I never really called him anything but "Mister" maybe once or twice. He seemed to be nice, and looked very gentlemanly, very tall and not bad looking - she had my blessing.

I didn't mind when he was around, even though I had to sleep in the kitchen on the rickety canvas bed. But I was very happy to be going out with him and grandma everyday. It was the first time I watched a movie in the cinema, (I didn't remember what the film was about) and then to eat out at various "restaurants", more like food stands really, with a skinny table and a few stools to sit on, but the food was always delicious and plentiful. In fact, besides making tea and toasting corn, I did not recall seeing my grandma did much of any other cooking. We ate out or had "take-away" for the whole of my stay. I was totally happy during that week, so much talking, so much laughter, the movies, eating out, just my grandmother, her boyfriend, and me. It was perfect!

On my last evening, we went to hear the local opera playing a story that I later found out was based on "Carmen". I thought the singing was good though nothing sounded like Bizet's Carmen, but I hated the story then and didn't think much of the characters either, and I still don't like the opera Carmen very much now. Perhaps because it was also the last day of my stay with my grandmother and not long after that she got sick and died, I saw "Mister" crying at her funeral.

Somehow I survived at least ten difficult years of schooling and poor health. It was a dazed sort of existence even though I seemed to be popular socially among some relatives, friends and foes alike. As for "love" and the opposite sex, all were insignificant, passing by without leaving any lasting impression either physically or emotionally. At the age of twenty-one I was quite indifferent to most of anything and anyone that I'd encountered. I had many "friends" but none I desired or considered "close". No one I either envied or admired. Until one day, when this 26-year-old man came into my life, he who brought another world to me, the world that was in my imagination ever since so long ago.

France 1968

1968 was the year of the Monkey, which I remembered so clearly because it was the year that the city of Saigon was attacked by the communist fighters. It was known as: the "Tet Offensive"

I was in France on a holiday, a young girl walking along Boulevard St Germaine in Paris 6th arrondissement, and one morning in July I was shocked to witness the destruction of the street from anti-war demonstrations in the month of May that same year: The "Sorbonne crisis" which I was told about by some friends. I had not had the time or the chance to grow up yet and was looking forward to experiencing life, I had no desire to think of either war or peace, nor letting either subject concern me.

Most of our time was spent in France, Switzerland and Italy. My mother and I then travelled through New York and Los Angeles staying only a few days in each place and continuing onto the Pacific areas: Tahiti, New Caledonia, then Sydney where we spent a whole week touring the cities of Sydney and Canberra with a very nice young taxi driver who also studied Law at Sydney University. Through this young law student/taxi driver, I learnt about Australian National Service Scheme, known as "conscription": Twenty-year-old men were required to register for the draft, then were subject to a ballot in which, if their birth date was drawn, they would have to do their service in the army and be liable for combat duties in Vietnam. My friend, the law student, was glad his birth date was not drawn, but he had good friends who were at that moment fighting in Vietnam. It was like a lottery you would not want to win.

In September 1968 we made a quick stop in Singapore at a small hotel for couple of nights before flying back to Saigon. At Singapore airport about to board an Air Vietnam flight, among the crowd, a couple of Americans whom I knew happened to board the same flight: one from the Associated Press, the other from Reuters Press Agency, through them I met this Australian reporter. While each man offered to carry one of my many bags, only one remained faithfully carrying them through our many journeys for the rest of his life. Until one morning in April 2015 when he took his last breath in my arms. His name was Brian Peck. He was my best friend, my confidant, and my all. He brought happiness into my everyday life for 45 years. I could not imagine how I would do without him, but one thing for sure I knew was that, he was the only person in this world that I have ever loved, and that love was not a perfumed pillow.

Gulf of Tonkin, off Nth Viet.
Boarding the Australian
destroyer, "HOBART" Sept '68

Interview with President Thieu

Brian obtained a scoop interview with President Thieu after the My-Lai's massacre; it was picked up by Reuters, run by NZ Press and one of the big American Television networks. Apparently, a major American news agency called him to ask how the Australian Broadcasting Corporation managed to obtain this exclusive interview on such a story.

Assignments In Vietnam

Brian talked of some dangerous situations on his assignments in Vietnam:

"...The first assignment after reaching Saigon during the period of fighting, I was very new and didn't know which were incoming shots – coming towards us – and which were "outgoing" fired by our people and going away from us, but the important thing was to get it recorded. I looked down over the parapet of the roof and saw into a room where a Chinese family was cowering back against the wall. One floor above them I saw a man clutching his stomach. Looking more closely, I realised he was clutching his sides, not with p.a.i.n, but with laughter. In the mist of all that was happening, he had tossed a string of firecrackers down to the room below, terrifying the family, and he thought this was funny. It may sound a crazy incident, but in some ways it typifies the attitude of some of the people. Fighting has become so much a part of their lives, that there is still a joke to be had in the midst of it, though at that time perhaps a somewhat unfortunate joke. The sound of firecrackers came onto my tape and added to the firing.

When things quietened down a bit I had time to develop more of the economic and political side of the story, and try to find answers to the important question of why these things were taken place. This was my job for the rest of the time – covering the war, but not necessarily going to all the fighting.

There are unfortunate accidents sometime. A plane I was in on the central coast had a malfunction and dropped one of its bombs of napalm into the paddy field below us, where peasants were working. Later, there was another malfunction and rockets fired accidentally, so we went out to try and drop the remaining bombs and rockets into the sea. All but one came off and was jettisoned into the sea, but this rocket was left hanging by a clip, primed and ready to go off. As we were coming in, very coolly the Vietnamese pilot told the control tower, and the Americans declares it an emergency, prevented all other aircraft from landing, cleared the runways and alerted fire brigade and ambulance. It was most disconcerting landing with the rocket waggling on the wing and the fire engines and ambulance waiting, but we made it safely..."

Brian's tour of duty ended, he returned to Australia in December 1969. In February 1970, with my Pan Am ticket and all I ever possessed inside a medium-sized suitcase I boarded the plane that stopped over in Singapore where I rested for a couple of nights before my destination: Sydney, Australia.

Bernard Joseph, an ABC journalist that Brian worked with when he was stationed in Saigon met me in Singapore. It was arranged for me to lodge at the flat of Neil Davis, a Visnews' cameraman who was also working with Brian in Saigon. Neil was away at the time, his amah (whose name I don't remember) looked after me during my short stay.

I cried a little on my first night sleeping in a strange house on a strange bed. I missed my siblings only a little but I did not miss my parents at all. Their verbal abuse in the attempt to stop me from leaving during the last three weeks echoed in my head so strong and clear that I almost had to pinch myself to remind me that I was no longer in my parents' house. An emotion of relief flooded through my whole being, my little heart relaxed and I went to sleep thinking very soon I would be reunited with my lover. I did not love nor hate my parents though I was always grateful that I was born from them and I tried to be dutiful and obliging at the best of times, even if I was void of any feeling towards them. "Indifference" I guess, would be the word to describe my feeling.

Saigon 1969

Since our first encounter at Singapore airport, Brian and I saw each other as often as we could. It was not "love at first sight", life was difficult in the increasingly urgent tempo of the war, despite that our relationship developed slowly. Brian was still not legally divorced from his first marriage and I, with all my insecurity of a sheltered life, had never experienced anything but fear, though that did not stop me from kissing a few frogs before I met Brian. Although Brian never thought much of my kissing, he taught me how instead. The Vietnam War saw some of our friends lose their lives. I remembered distinctively seeing François Sully, Richard Merron and Sean Flynn who often returned from battles, laden with camera gear looking exhausted except for Sean, who I could still see so clearly; always a big grin on his face. He and Brian were at the same age. Then, I had no idea he was Errol Flynn's son, nor who Errol Flynn was? Their jobs were not fighting in the war but reporting the battles.

My family treated Brian with enough friendliness when he came calling, but they were very much against the idea of any further development in our relationship. Behind the scenes, they gave me a very hard time when I continued seeing Brian and refused any dates my mother arranged for me. If they could they would have locked me up but my determination somehow deterred their action. I was not a religious person, not to the religion I was born into, but I always believed I had a guardian angel that looked after me, perhaps more than one.

It was a warm Wednesday in early February of my arrival, welcoming me at Sydney airport a bearded man called out: *"Darling!"* I walked right past him without looking while my eyes were scanning the arrival terminal searching for my lover's face. Again: *"Darling, darling!"* The voice sounded familiar, I turned around to the bearded man and he smiled at me with his eyes. A moment passed, our eyes met and held... then I ran into his arms, we kissed and his beard tickled my face. He did not have a beard when we said goodbye in Saigon a couple of months earlier, I did not recognise him.

Sydney 1971

He kept the beard for seven years. During that time we got married, our son was born and Brian left the ABC. We moved to Canberra where he worked as Information and Press Attaché for Australian Embassies and we were soon on our first posting to Indonesia. Dick Woolcott was the ambassador in Jakarta at the time. Jakarta was then rated a 'difficult' post but we managed to survive by learning the language before we arrived. It made our lives a little easier to understand and be understood. Thank goodness Bahasa Indonesian wasn't a difficult language to learn. The invasion of East Timor by Indonesia in 1975 brought back memories of war and conflict in Vietnam and Brian was on the reverse role as one of our journalist friends stated: "From the poacher to the game-keeper". During our years in Jakarta, we saw the visits of two Australian Prime Ministers: First was Gough Whitlam with Jim Cairns, (his much talked about deputy) and Ms Junie Morosi.

(The whole story between Jim Cairns and Junie Morosi's relationship came full circle published by The Age in 2002 in which the journalist compared with the situation between Bill Clinton and Monica Lewinsky.)

Whitlam's reign was short, the country decided on Malcolm Fraser, known as the PM with the razor gang and famous quote: "There is no such thing as a free lunch." And of course, we all know about the "Dismissal." Politically, it was a very interesting time. Our first posting opened our eyes to the good, the bad and the ugly in the Diplomatic Corps, which we could have never imagined otherwise. Perhaps being the "poacher" might have been a little nicer. However to recall our time in Jakarta I would have had to write in a different chapter.

Jakarta 1974

The end of the Vietnam War brought my husband back to Saigon in a more daring mission. He was to rescue my mother and my youngest brother out of the country. In the last week of April leading up to Anzac Day we gathered from the news on Jakarta's television and Radio Australia that, the situation was becoming more and more hopeless for the South Vietnamese Government and the people were starting to panic. I talked to my mother via telephone from Jakarta, but the line was so bad that it was hard to hear each other (Indonesia, at the time was still very backward in communications technology.) I took my 2-year-old son with me, we flew to Singapore hoping to have better communication with my family and to learn what really happened regarding my sponsorship documents for my mother, a younger sister and brother to join me in Australia. (My father died three years earlier)

I learned that the Australian Embassy in Saigon would only take my mother and my sister out of the country. For complicated diplomatic reasons they could not include my brother who was at the age for military service in S. Vietnam. Naturally, my mother refused to leave without her youngest son. My sister left on the last flight out of Saigon with the ambassador on Anzac Day. Through duty and obligation I was ready to come into Saigon to help my family but Brian would not hear of it for he was fearful that I should fail and thus not be able to get out myself. He decided to go instead.

In Jakarta, Brian asked the embassy permission to travel to Saigon but was refused. Against orders he chose to leave on Anzac Day (as it was his day of holiday) in the hope that he would just fly into Saigon, pick up my family and immediately get back out on a return flight to be back in Jakarta within a day.

To prepare, he carried a bunch of $US tucked in his belt in case he needed to bribe the airport officials.

Later he recalled: As the last Air Vietnam flight landed on "Tan Son Nhut" airport, he could see the Australian Ambassador's plane taking off which meant there was no more diplomatic connection with S. Vietnam and with his diplomatic passport, he was actually the only representative there. Once off the plane he also learnt that there would be no more flights out of Saigon. The airport was closed for all commercial flights.

During the next two days, I lost all contact with Saigon, I could not talk to my husband or my family, all I could do was just glue my eyes to the English language news on Singapore television. I was in agony, feeling so guilty that I sent my husband to danger without thinking if anything would happen to him. Meanwhile the announcer on the news read: "Saigon has surrendered to the communist force..."

Soon the phone rang; an ABC journalist based in Singapore who we knew asked if he could bring a shortwave radio over for me to listen and translate a news item for him, including a speech by a South Vietnam caretaker president. As all communication had shut down from Saigon, he thought with my help he could file this story to Australia. I did as best as I could while praying that someone up there would protect my husband.

The following day the phone rang: It was Brian calling from US Clark Field airbase in Manila; he had managed to get my mother and brother out of Saigon! He was my hero! But more important he was safe. In a happy relieved state of mind and perhaps from a few sleepless nights worrying without much eating, I fainted and felt flat on my face cutting my upper lip on one of my son's Matchbox car lying on the floor. When Brian actually saw me back home in Jakarta he exclaimed: *"Oh my darling, you looked as though you came out of the war and not me... ha, ha..."*

Brian came back to the office on his return. He was scolded severely by the ambassador and the minister for leaving his post without permission. Among his colleagues, some people raised their eyebrows in contempt; others shook his hand with approval. How he got my family out was another story altogether.

Messages written by some colleagues soon after Brian died:

1- *"It was while in Jakarta that Brian gave embassy mates, including Ambassador Dick Woolcott, a few anxious days when he mysteriously disappeared. But he returned after a short time. In a highly dangerous exercise he had managed to get into Vietnam as the Communist forces took over and was able to rescue his Vietnamese mother and brother-in-law from what could have been a nasty fate."*

2- *"I was in Manila at the time of the fall of Saigon and got a late night phone call from Brian who had arrived out of the blue at the huge (US) Clark Air Base north of Manila with his mother-in-law and, as I recall, a brother-in-law. They had fled with virtually nothing. Jacqui and I collected some emergency supplies and headed north. It took a while to find them — a USIS guy I knew had been sent there because of the media interest, gave us a hand and we eventually found them in a huge hangar with many hundreds of other refugees. They were totally traumatised. Unfortunately, because Australia agreed with the Philippines' policy of pretending the South Vietnamese who were being processed through their country didn't exist, we couldn't get an entry permit for Brian and family. When I next saw him - years later - Brian told me they had been flown by the US Air Force to Guam and from there they were able to get the appropriate paperwork to get to Australia."*

3- "I first met Brian Peck in early 1975 when he was appointed First Secretary (Information) at the Australian Embassy in Jakarta, Indonesia. I was the Deputy Head of Mission.

Brian occupied a central place in the Embassy. What impressed me from the outset was his enthusiastic approach to his work and his keen desire to contribute to the strengthening of ties between Australia and Indonesia.

Brian was devoted to his family and made a brave journey to Saigon just before the fall of the city into the hands of North Vietnam in order to take Thai's mother to safety. Many consider this to be a heroic act by Brian.

I shall always remember Brian for his kindness, cheerfulness and devotion to his family and for his important work for Australia."

Rescue Mission

"*Why took you so long?*" My mother said when Brian arrived at the house, even before she greeted him with a "Hello". Brian's reply was that he tried to get there as quick as he could.

On his way from Jakarta he could not be any quicker. Brian had to make a stop in Singapore to change flight. His Air Vietnam's ticket was booked waiting for him to collect at the airline's counter. He did not even have time to see our son and me while we were waiting in Singapore. He carried no luggage but just the clothes he was in and his passport (there was no mobile phone). He only managed to make a call from the public phone. We talked briefly trying to comfort each other. I was not just worried about my family but I was very concerned for my husband's safety.

According to Brian, the city was in a solemn atmosphere though business was going on as usual. He trusted no one and it looked like each for his own to find the way of fleeing from Saigon. His aim was to take my mother and my younger brother out of the country whichever way he could. He did not want to communicate with anyone, not even with my two other brothers, one was an officer in the army, the other was a deserter who came out because he gathered it was then safe to show himself. Neither of them had much feeling toward my husband either good or bad. Brian had a very uneasy overnight sleeping in my mother's house. He could not wait till the early hour of the morning.

As Brian already knew there was no Australian representative in the country. The only other Australian Brian knew was our friend Visnews cameraman Neil Davis who had no intention of leaving Saigon. He stayed to be the first to witness number 843 tank crashing through the gate of the Presidential Palace (where Brian interviewed President Thieu in 1969.)

Although, my mother possessed all the appropriate documents for Australia and my sponsorship papers, she gave them all to my sister who left the country the day before with the Australian ambassador and his staff. All that my mother had was just the photo I sent to her of our wedding (when Brian put the ring on my finger). Brian took the photo from her and put it in his pocket.

Brian's first and probably the only thought was to head to the US embassy to seek some help as he thought since Australia had been "all the way with Lyndon B. Johnson" (once declared by Harold Holt, Australian Prime Minister who disappeared while swimming at Cheviot Beach December 1967. Brian was one of the first reporters at the scene when he was asked to read a statement for the television news.) Though Brian was not sure how, he hoped the American embassy would help him in some ways. At the embassy, Brian was let in without any problem because he was a white European, while outside people lined up in the heat waiting for their turns, perhaps they had been waiting for days. At the consulate desk, after hearing Brian's request, a heavy American female clerk said loudly:

"How do I know these people are your relatives, have you any proof?"

A moment of thought and Brian pulled our wedding photo from his pocket:

"Actually, this is my wife who is the daughter and sister of my mother and brother-in-law." Said he.

She laughed and said: *"Actually... That's so cute!"* After a quick study of the photograph, she instructed him to come back with his relatives as soon as possible and then she would see how she could help them. That morning my youngest brother was at the lycée sitting for his Baccalauréat. My mother was packing while waiting, she would have had taken all the things she wanted in about three suitcases or more but Brian's advice to her: "less is better in the present circumstances." He anxiously waited while kept urging her to make haste. So down to one suitcase full of her photographs and glamorous Vietnamese costumes. As soon as my brother returned from his exam, all three left for the US embassy. (My brother later on found out from a friend that he did pass that exam.)

Almost the whole afternoon sitting in the US embassy, my husband and my family waited to hear how they were to travel to the airport. Brian was impatiently going back and forth getting the attention of anyone whom he thought might help, who were also trying their best to help not just him but many others as well. During a conversation Brian found out that these people had great difficulties looking for the way to transport half a dozen Vietnamese/American orphan babies whose holding proper passports and visas to travel to the US but without any minders. In quick thinking Brian seized the chance to get himself and my family to the airport by volunteered his help taking the babies. When his suggestion was accepted. He negotiated with the consulate to provide him the necessary transport. By then it was getting toward the evening and things had to be done before nightfall. Finally it was arranged for Brian, my mother and my 17-year-old brother to carry half a dozen babies getting into a large American car driven by a Vietnamese driver with a US Marine carrying a big gun for escort heading for "Tan Son Nhut" where a Hercules aircraft was waiting. They had to travel through some military checkpoints but Brian kept urging the driver to keep on driving at normal speed without stopping, they managed to arrive at the airport unscathed. My brother was glad to get out of the car as he later recalled: it seemed like an eternity hiding underneath all the babies with their smelly nappies. The babies were handed over to the American nurses who took care of changing and feeding them. Afterward all were on board the aircraft as it was getting dark and the communist forces began to shell the airport with rockets. So back to the waiting and more waiting until the shelling finished before they could take off. The aircraft they were in was fortunate not to get hit while some others did.

The next day they landed at Clark Field Airbase in The Philippines among thousands of other refugees. Everyone was exhausted but no one complaint even the babies. Brian recalled: One of the babies he carried was fascinated with his hairy arm and tried to pull the hair off one by one yet, he didn't even feel the pain! They were glad to have some food and drinks and realised they had nothing to eat or drink since leaving home from Saigon after breakfast the day before. Brian told me he was glad that he insisted on going into Saigon to help my family and did not let me. He could not imagine how I would have managed to get out, if I had gone into the country with our son.

***

Our posting in Jakarta continued on for another two years and our daughter was born in 1977. A few months later, we left Jakarta to return to Australia. We took a couple of weeks holidays in Bali on the way back. One humid afternoon

Brian told us that he would go out for a swim, the children and I were happy to take our siesta in the cool of the hotel bungalow. I was resting on the couch in the living room; half awake after a heavy shut-eye, the sort of sleep that you sometimes wake up from wondering whether you are asleep or awake. As I was trying to open my eyes I could see a figure standing in the room looking as though he was smiling. I thought perhaps I was dreaming so I shut my eyes and went back to sleep, thinking at the same time that it was a weird dream, could it be a stranger really came into my room and why did he just stand and smile? I opened my eyes again; this person was still there with that same familiar smile. Puzzling over the scene I tried harder to wake myself out of slumber and thought to myself, "I knew that smile! That loving, gentle smile!" Then I sat right up and said, "Oh my god! It's YOU!" He had his beard shaved off. At that time our 4 year-old son woke up from his afternoon nap, came out of the bedroom, rubbing his eyes. Looking at his dad he said matter of factly, *"You looked like a guest."* Brian did it again: Caught me by surprise! And how I loved kissing his face without the beard. I made him promise not to grow it again and since then, we sometime referred to that as our seven years itch that needed to be shaved off.

Resuming life back in the Australian climate after three and half years in Indonesia was quite refreshing. Our humble home in an ordinary suburb in Canberra was a lot smaller but a lot cozier and we were very happy to be just us without any domestic helper running around. It was not long before Brian was told to take up another posting to the United States and though our little cosy domesticity was being disrupted, we were quite happy to pack up and be on the move again.

A week before our departure to Washington, while Brian was staying back in Canberra for the last few days finishing his work, I took our children to Sydney to say goodbye to my mother, the children's grandmother. I happened to visit the first film set in Sydney located at the Sydney show-ground in a suburb not far from where my mother lived. There, the assistant director and the staging team proudly shown me a made-up Vietnamese village, for a backdrop in a feature film called "The odd angry shot". It was authentic enough although I have never encountered any village with so much wet black mud on the ground. To keep the thick black substance moist for the light reflection, they had to keep hosing it with water. From the little that I knew, muddy areas like that were usually found on rice paddies. I have seen many villages not far from the city, and though poor the pavements were relatively clean, even if the concrete was badly sealed. A young assistant took a fancy to me. He asked if I would like to be in the film as an extra. It took me only a short moment to accept but I told him I'd have to leave for Washington at the weekend. He told me the shooting would be starting in the morrow and I was just in time. With another look at the wet muddy ground, I told him that I would not like to walk in all that mud. He asked, *"Where would you like to be?"* I pointed to a cute "Romeo & Juliet" balcony: *"That's where"*. A big grin broke out on the young man's face as he said, *"Do you know that's where the Saigon bargirls stand? Is that where you want to be?"* Without any hesitation I replied, *"Sure, why not!"* *"Do you know we could not convince any Vietnamese young woman to play the role, we had to pick a Chinese and a Malaysian student to do the job?"* said he. I told him I had no problem pretending. He asked to me go out for a drink afterwards, I told him I was married and no, I was not a bargirl. Shooting of the scene took place the next day. I brought the children along and the film crew took pleasure in looking after them while their mother was being made-up to resemble a bargirl. Then avoiding the muddy area, I was led to the 'cute' balcony for my two-second famous role. My job was to pretend to puff a cigarette and to smile and wave at the GI. During the course of the day, another assistant approached me, he asked if I was willing to say a few words and perhaps take my blouse off! I could earn a few hundred dollars more. I told them that was far enough as my adventure went. I hadn't even told my husband yet what I just did.

1978

On the plane en-route to Washington Brian laughed when I told him: *"Oh darling, The State Department may think that the wife of an Australian diplomat is a bargirl..."* Well, who cares, I just didn't want to walk in all that mud. It was not just a puddle in which one could see one's reflection but in the thick black mud that one could see no-where. I no longer had any desire to step into a puddle or wished to be anywhere else. I had Brian and thus my world and destiny had already embraced me and I was too busy nurturing my dream, as it became reality.

Our posting in the US lasted almost six years. From Washington we were posted to San Francisco where our children grew very much into little Americans. Brian was working hard and often travelling interstate but we still managed to make it an enjoyable and memorable post. We loved the America we knew, the friends we made across the country and all the beauty of the country itself that we were lucky enough to visit. We could have stayed on in the US indefinitely. Brian was offered a job with the World Bank in Washington at the end of our term. The temptation was enormous but after thinking it through we chose to return to Australia; even though neither Brian nor I were born here, we felt a strong pull toward this country.

"Uluru" Watercolour

"... A sunburnt country of sweeping plains and ragged mountains. Of droughts and flooding rains..."

Dorothea Mackellar

And yes, we came to love this land and we did not regret our decision. Meanwhile our children grew up and eventually chose their own families, had their own children and made their homes in the US and the UK. Living their destiny.

Brian wrote of his feeling when he visited the Northern Territory in 1996, which very much echoed my feeling of a brief visit to Uluru in 2016.

"... After living in Australia for much of my adult life, reading about Indigenous Australians, seeing and appreciating their art

and beginning to understand the huge issues confronting the original inhabitants, I knew something was missing.

But what was it? How could I find an answer if I wasn't sure of the question? After visiting Uluru and Kata Tjuta and talking with their traditional owners the question began to form in my head. Their quietly expressed passion and carefully polite discussion of what their land means to them made the question clearer.

As I entered Kakadu I wondered if I was being led – gently pushed, tugged one way and then another. Was it the spirits of the Bininj and Mungguy people of Kakadu who were coercing me, showing me where to find the answer to my question?

The answer was at Ubir. At first I could only see the Nourlangie Rock standing out of the plain. Then I explored galleries of rock paintings of fish and animals created not hundreds of years ago, not thousands but 20,000, 30,000 or 40,000 years past. This was my answer. I was a guest in the home of the world's oldest living culture."

Brian Peck

***

The last twenty years of Brian's life were the happiest years we shared, the sort of happiness that wiped out, all the ups and downs, the discords and despairs of the past. In between growing up, marriage, children, and searching for the meaning of life. I could not say we have mastered anything, though I have learnt enormously and have found a certain peace within my mind and soul and I was perfectly happy with the experience and the knowledge I gathered, it has been more than I have ever hoped. How lucky Brian and I were that we still had each other to have and to hold, enough time for us to be young again. To be the lovers we were at the beginning of time without any hang-ups, but with the love and trust we had for each other. In the last twenty years we did not have to gaze at the horizon. We were content just to look at each other, we grew closer than ever with our bodies and our souls but time did not stand still for us...

My childhood puddle had taken me so much further than I could ever imagine. The man who brought me a world full of love and tenderness has now gone and time did not bring me any relief. I miss him at the drop of a coin. I miss him as the rain is falling and while the sun is about to rise. I miss him in the light of day and shadow of night.

"You are still not much of a kisser, are you?" He told me a few days before he died when I kissed his cheek, a long inhale as if I wanted to breathe in as much as my breath allowed, the sweet scent of his skin.

After a heavy rain, from the overflowing gutters, which flooded the rainwater tank, water came racing down onto an already muddy garden, forming a huge puddle. I walked around as not to step into it lest I spoil the pretty reflection of the sky above.

Reflection

Chelsea beach 2016

"I thought of you and how you love this beauty,
And walking up the long beach all alone
I heard the waves breaking in measured thunder.
As you and I once heard their monotone.

Around me were the echoing dunes, beyond me
The cold and sparkling silver of the sea --
We two will pass through death and ages lengthen
Before you hear that sound again with me."

Sarah Teasdale

2

Love unto Love

"Sunset on the bay" Oil on canvas

"...Love possesses not nor would it be possessed. For love is sufficient unto love..."

Kahlil Gibran

To be born at all was difficult enough.

To be born through the physical pain caused to another human being evokes quite an amazing feeling of gratitude, and I am forever being grateful even if I held no affection toward the woman who gave birth to me, especially when she had to go through it six more times. I never once regretted my feeling. Once in a while in the past when my mother was alive, I sent her a card on my birthday thanking her for giving birth to me. She never acknowledged it and she never wished me happy birthday either. I was not born out of love.

In our younger years when my only sister and I used to talk, we wondered how would we have turned out if we had grown up nurtured with love. My sister came to a conclusion that she must have been an adopted child because if our parents were her "real" parents, she would have had felt their love. For myself, I wished that a loving couple that loved me enough to adopt me had done so.

> *"... Your children are not your children. They are the sons and daughters of Life's longing for itself. They come from through but not from you. And though they are with you yet they belong not to you..."*

In 1941 across the other side of the globe in Saint Albans, England a baby boy was born out of wedlock he was placed in an orphanage. We would never know what were the circumstances of the time. We only knew that he was named "John Hurson" at his birth on a fine spring morning.

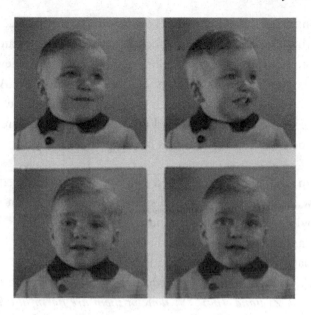

A Mrs Peck who lived on Beech Road in St Albans came to the orphanage almost daily, giving the baby boy and other orphans the mother's care and affection that were much needed. Her job was a volunteer foster mother but her daily contact with John wasn't just a job, it was a love and devotion until one day she just could not leave him behind. Mr and Mrs Peck adopted him and John became Brian Marcus Peck. Brian was loved in abundance, as if his destiny was to be born out of love in the middle of the time when England and Europe were under a cloud of war. Something as beautiful as "love" came out of war.

At the end of the war peace came, also came the divorce of his adopted parents. Some years later his mother remarried to Mr A. Sears, Brian called him "Alfs". Alf was a kind and gentle person who provided for Brian and his mother not just the material needs but with all the love and care they needed for the rest of time and in which Brian was always grateful throughout his life. When Christine Williams interviewed Brian for her book "Fathers & Sons" he said: "At Alfs' funeral – I wept right through the service. He meant much more to me as a father than I'd let on. I have wondered – maybe even hoped that I was his illegitimate son."

Brian and his mother joined Mr Sears who migrated to New Zealand from England some years before. Brian was growing up in New Zealand until the age of 21 when he came to settle in Australia. On my first visit to New Zealand Alfs took me on a tour around a seaside town near Auckland, he told me: "*We have many strange creatures here in New Zealand Thai, but none of them are harmful except the human.*" I adored him! I could listen to his lifelong story forever and would never be tired of it. He had a dry sense of humour with a dash of cynicism about people in general and politics in particular. As a young man he travelled widely and wrote beautifully, he was also a great embroider and rug weaver. I was fortunate enough to be given one of his best works.

"Langleys" Silk Embroidery

We were living in Bethesda, MD during our posting in Washington when six months after the death of Brian's mother. Alfs decided to visit England via the US. We were delighted that he came to stay with us for a few weeks. It was a great opportunity for our children to have a much better connection almost exclusively with their "grandfather" Alfs was the only grandpa figure that our kids had ever known. He would spend hours telling the children all sorts of stories by the fireplace, it was the most heartwarming scene for me to witness - It brought happy tears to my eyes thinking of the childhood I did not have.

With grandpa 1980

Be that as it may, I have long forgiven my parents for the way they treated me. From the day I left my parents' home, I started to shed the skin I was born into and have moved forward in my life without a backward glance. It took me many more years to overcome my nightmares. With Brian and his tender love by my side, I also gradually shed my fear. There was no need for me to harbour any resentment toward my parents, who I came to understand did not know any better, I considered myself very lucky indeed to have been born. Perhaps I should be thankful as well as grateful to my parents, and that if I have been brought up with love and nurturing, I might have turned out to be a real brat!

On the other side Brian used to say that he was the lucky one to have found me. However our 45 years together were not all roses. As with any other union Brian and I went through some difficult times throughout our marriage. We came together with our love though so strong, yet we were two very different individuals with different background, language and culture. Strong opposites also meant heavy crashes when the temper flared. Brian was very stubborn but he was a lot calmer and more logical than I could ever be. As for me, Brian used to tease by calling me "the bag he picked up at Singapore airport" or his

"Saigon's souvenir!" He said he was destined to fall in love with me – the whole kit and caboodle: "my temper, my frankness, my serious dark eyes, my flat little nose and even the scent of my tears, a taste would turn him on..." I still couldn't figure that out but he is no longer around for me to "interrogate".

Blue Mountain

I remembered during our first year living together we often argued about insignificant little things. One evening, after a sort of a tiff, Brian went out for a drink with some mates and came home late while I was asleep. He came to bed as quiet as a mouse managed not to wake me at all. In the morning, he slept in while I was up dressed and ready for the day. When I decided to have a piece of toast with my cup of tea I could not find a knife anywhere to spread the butter, I had to use a fork instead. I woke him up and asked him what happened to the knives? He got up off the bed, put his hand under the mattress and a whole bunch of knives and the chopsticks started to roll out. I could not help but laugh, what ever he did, he must have felt pretty worried.

He said: *"You never know what the Asian would do to you using chopsticks!"*

I told him: *"We have our w...a...y...s!"*

And we made up...

***

"The First Kiss with Robert Redford"

(My little "creative" writing from our reminiscence of the first time Brian and I exchanged our first kiss)

"It had been raining steadily all day; the sky was dark and threatening. At times, the heavens opened and the rain came rushing down over the roofs of houses, filled up the gutters in a bursting torrent emptying itself on the ground turning the walkway into mud.

He walked as fast as he could, his small umbrella turned inside out as the gust passed through, he wondered why he bothered to carry it as he could feel the wetness taking over his shirt and soaking into his skin. He was on his way to a press conference, though it was more like press propaganda from the government military press agent, trying to pacify the media both at home and abroad.

The whole town was grey with heavy warm air, every house absorbed humidity like a sponge, and inside the cafe where he stopped for a cuppa, the wall soaked up moisture like sweat, while a single air-con through the hole on the wall was groaning on full speed.

He saw her, their eyes met; she gave him her brightest smile and he said to himself: "Oh, my god! She looks so young." They had been out a few times, always together with some of their friends but they had not yet been alone. He thought she liked him as much as he liked her by the way she looked at him with those beautiful serious dark eyes. A song he heard somewhere.

> *"...Drink to me, only with thine eyes*
> *And I will pledge with mine;*
> *Or leave a kiss but in the cup,*
> *And I'll not look for wine.*
> *The thirst that from the soul doth rise*
> *Doth ask a drink divine:*
> *But might I of Jove's nectar sup*
> *I would not change for thine."*

Ben Jonson (1572-1637)

She was nursing her ice coffee at the table by the window, through its foggy glass panel the street scene outside looked like an impressionist painting. Her smiling eyes looked up at him and how he wanted to gather her in his arms and kiss her but he dared not.

Even though she was well educated, and had travelled the world with her mother as a chaperon, she came from a strict family. One and twenty, looking as though in her late teen, he thought. Meanwhile he was married with a three years old son whom he loved and adored, his wife had recently moved in with her lover. They were not yet divorced and he could not bring himself to think about that at the moment, although he was missing his son every single day since he'd been away.

What madness to even thinking about courting this young woman when he did not have any idea how his future would work out. Yet, he fell for her, in "Like" as he did not want to touch the word "Love", for his delicate soul that would be too sacred a word to use it loosely. No, not yet, maybe not ever. He might be killed in a battle somewhere during his assignment here. Or was it just an excuse to avoid a commitment? *A bit drastic, isn't it!* He said to himself chasing the thought away.

He drank his cold black coffee in one gulp and told her that he had to attend a press conference but maybe they could meet again later to see a movie perhaps? Walking away smiling he thought: What a brilliant idea! We could sit right at the back and it would be an opportunity for the first kiss...

(And we did meet again to see a film that starred with Robert Redford and Natalie Wood. The film was dubbed in French with Vietnamese subtitle so Brian could only understand the story through the movie's actions and mere guessing but he was

quite happy sitting there cuddled me in his arms and that was the day we exchanged our first kiss. I later told Brian that it was also the first time I set eye on the actor Robert Redford and I thought he was so handsome, I wasn't sure whether I fell in love with Robert Redford or with Brian Peck and his kiss on that day, or "both"? With all the guys I kissed before I met Brian, he did not seem to care, but he was quite jealous with Robert Redford. Poor Mr. Redford! He didn't even know me yet, to be resented by my husband for all those years.)

"...You shall be together when the white wings of death scatter your days. But let there be spaces in your togetherness. And let the winds of heaven dance between you..."

22 December 1971

We gave ourselves to each other in marriage, not in the traditional way although Brian was quite proper and that he wrote a note asking my parents for my hand. I told him it was not necessary because I already gave myself to him but he insisted on doing the right thing. My father wrote only to me expressing how disappointed he was, that I did not consider coming home to get married at the cathedral in Saigon. I did not reply to him and I did not care whether he approved or not. My parents never gave us their blessings. There was no announcement and my siblings were never told. Brian and I went ahead with our plan: No church, no chapel, no relatives, no official nor tradition. We happily walked to the Sydney Registrar Office with a couple of friends for witnesses. Brian proudly ticked "none" on declaring his religion, I wrote down: born Catholic became "none". So we were both "none" since.

Though we don't believe in any religion we were not exactly agnostic or atheist. Brian's parents were Church of England without much churchgoing and did not force their children into any religion. My parents on the other side strictly adhered to the Catholic Church in Vietnam: Mass in the early hour of every morning and confession every Friday so you could receive communion for the following week. Hail Mary every evening's prayer and "stations of the cross" 3 times a day at Easter. And if you didn't do as expected, you would be punished severely. As a youngster, I could not work out what sin I should commit so I confessed all the seven sins that I read in the Catholic bible, thus insuring I was absolved from all of them. My mother took me to the Vatican in the hope that if I should be blessed by the Pope then, I would be inspired to enter a convent and be married to God, which should make her the proudest mother on earth.

"... Your daily life is your temple and your religion. When you enter into it take with you your all. The things you have fashioned in necessity or for delight. For in reverie you cannot rise above your achievements nor fall lower than your failures. And take with you all men: For in adoration you cannot fly higher than their hopes nor humble yourself lower than their despair. And if you would know god, be not there for a solver of riddles..."

Pope Paul VI

To Rome we went, like any other tourists we took each other's photo with the handsome Swiss Guard outside a tall ornate gate of the palace, what a job! It would have required much disciplines imagine you can't even blink an eye while some silly young woman tried a staring contest at you. At the entrance we were invited to take a stroll in the Vatican garden while waiting for our turn. It was a sight of a total neatness that I have never seen anywhere and such a vast stretch of beautiful manicured lawn and shrubs, yet I would have preferred to see it a little untidier. A young man came directly toward me, stopped and introduced himself with a very heavy accent, I heard him but had no idea who he was, until he mentioned that he had the privilege to be in my photo and he admired my traditional dress. He was the Swiss Guard, not as handsome as when he was in his uniform. We conversed politely and he asked if we could meet for coffee. Before I could make up my mind a Vatican official came to guide us in for the audience with the Pope. I did not see that young man again and I could not find the photo either. It was all in the cloud!

I could boast that I had the privilege of shaking hands with the Pope (kissed his humongous ruby ring) and had a quick chat with him in a private audience, but that was all. I was more impressed with the richness of the Vatican, the grandeur of red velvet curtains and gold tassels draping from the high ceiling running from corridor after corridor, so magnificent! I wished I could dance a waltz along the shinning polished floor with a handsome beau. I was also in awed at the amazing architecture and the beauty of the world's famous artwork around St Peter's Basilica and of the city of Rome. Well, the Pope was kind enough to express his sympathy to us and to our country regarding the war that was going on.

Still, I had no desire to be any "nun", which disappointed my mother greatly. Her pathway to heaven appeared a bit harder to reach. I remembered my mother took me to visit a French convent when I was about 14 years old, her way of introducing me to the godliness of life. The convent was a beautiful building occupying the whole tranquil street in a leafy suburb. Surrounded by an enchanted garden, the mother superior was a beautiful French lady who spoke with such gentleness and softness in her voice. I could hear a lovely chant in the distance echoed by the sweet sound of chiming bells. The nuns in their habits moved around dark cloisters like shadows, they all looked so pretty and virginal. I was enchanted by the serenity of the whole atmosphere. But I said to my mother: *"No, I don't want to be a nun."* and *"Why do you want me to be a nun?"* Her reply was that she knew how hard life was to be a wife and a mother and then to have to go through the pain of childbirth. I could not imagine what childbirth pain was at the time but I told her that I would like to try it first. She was not pleased and while I was worrying what she would do next I also thought to myself, she went through childbirth seven times and she looked fine to me.

At seventeen, I was totally ignorant about the facts of life. My mother never talked to me about it even when she had already given up the thought of me entering the convent. It was something I did not dare to mention, as I knew it would anger my mother. I talked more to the maid, she was a married woman who once told me that she loved her wedding day and being in love was so romantic. My curiosity was aroused I asked: *"What about the wedding night?"* She said it was a bit painful, my mind thought immediately about childbirth but she said it was not the same thing. It was painful but "nice!"... What? Why did everything have to involve pain? (And I have always been an absolute "wuss" when it comes to physical pain.) Then, I thought I would have none of that.

I was a married woman at the age 24 living in Sydney though still an illegal immigrant on just a visitor's visa, which was running out. In the good old days, I could walk into the Immigration Department office in Sydney; smiled sweetly at the clerk and got my passport stamped every six months without any hassle. But I decided to get myself naturalized to become an "Aussie" and did away with the Vietnamese passport.

In Australia then, when it was quite simple to get naturalized. We went to the local mayor's office, filled out a form and made an appointment for a day when convenient to come along for a private ceremony. We lived in Bellevue Hill and Woollahra Council was situated in a suburb called Double Bay, a lovely spot by Sydney Harbour with a beautiful view. One lovely winter morning Brian and I arrived, we were served a cup of tea in beautiful fine china and a clerk came out, politely handled me a small bible and on which I should place my hand when I swore allegiance to Queen Elizabeth II of England. I told him: "*No, I am not swearing!*" He was quite apologetic for offending me as he thought perhaps something to do with my religion. At the same time he showed me the page that was inscribed with my name to mark the important day. I told him: "*That's okay, I shall keep the book for a souvenir but I am not going to swear on it.*" He was quite relieved and told me I could affirm the allegiance instead. The ceremony was brief though not lacking any pomp and circumstance. Afterward the mayor received us on the large terrace over looking the marvellous view with champagne and canapé - no flag, no vegemite sandwiches and no stuffed koala. It was quite civilised really. That was then, now it's a different ball-game altogether.

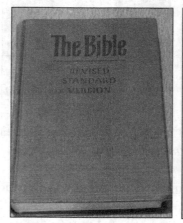 

"... You may give your children love but not your thoughts. For they have their own thoughts. You may house their bodies but not their souls. For their souls dwell in the house of tomorrow, which you cannot visit, not even in your dreams..."

Sydney January 1973

Our son was born the following year and Brian was over the moon! He was quite emotional when he saw the beautiful baby boy sleeping peacefully in the cot behind the viewing window, in the maternity ward at Crown Street Women's Hospital in Surrey Hills (which no longer exists). His tears wet my cheeks when he kissed me thanking me for giving him a son. I told him that I didn't do it all by myself. Then, we looked into each other eyes, through the tears we laughed, we shook our heads slowly saying together: "*No, it wasn't immaculate conception!*" Brian added: "*Thank goodness for that!*" It became a joke between us.

The childbirth pain had all disappeared by the time I held my son in my arms to nurse him and I was glad I had disappointed my mother. Yet to be fair, she later loved my children just like any grandmothers loved their grandkids.

It pleased me that she showed some affection even if I was not the receiver.

Besides giving birth I knew absolutely nothing else on the practical sides of life. I had no guidance from any one and no one to learn the ropes from. In the annex of the hospital we were settled in a lovely room overlooking the harbour, my baby and I were so well looked after for the whole week or maybe ten days. Then, I was not required to participate in anything like changing nappies or taking part in bathing the baby... etc. I thought it was pretty good - me floating around looking pretty – receiving visitors and being pampered by everyone for being so clever - having such a lovely baby. When it was time to come home I had a real shock at reality, but thank goodness I had Brian, he was the most devoted husband and father while still had had to go to work and I had never heard any complain from him. There was no such thing as "paternity leave" in those days. Five weeks later Brian's mother came over from New Zealand to help out. She stayed for three weeks and we had the best time together, when she held our baby in her arms tears welled up in her eyes, she told me her grandson was at the same age when she first held his dad. I thanked her for rescuing Brian from that orphanage, I could not imagine how my life would be if she didn't adopt him. It also warmed my heart witnessing the love Brian and his mother shared. Our baby son is now in his 40s, he has been living in England with his wife and his two daughters during the last ten years of his father's life. Brian and I did not have a chance to be near when his children were born.

I think I knew pain as much as I knew love.

"... For even as love crowns you so shall he crucify you. Even as he is for your love so is he for your pruning... Your pain is the breaking of the shell that encloses your understanding. And could you keep your heart in wonder at the daily miracles of your life, your pain would not seem less wondrous than your joy..."

In later years, Brian and I sometimes read "The Prophet" together, we often had great many times discussing the wisdom of Gibran and the meaning of life, death, religion... etc. (Often on a Sunday morning lying in bed.) Many times we agreed, and sometimes we didn't.

In the beginning of our wedded life we read "Love Story". It was a novel Brian gave me for our first wedding anniversary (based on just the title). He inscribed: *"Happy anniversary darling, we don't have to eat, we just read and make love..."* We didn't have money for expensive gifts, we didn't own a house, we lived in a rented flat but in one of the nicest suburbs in Sydney, we owned a cute little sport car and a nice little boat in which we enjoyed many outings cruising around the beautiful harbour. We went out to fine dining when came payday, the rest of time we ate mainly vegemite on toast and an apple a day. Sometimes Brian went out on his boat and managed to catch some fish but we never ate them, neither of us knew how to clean the fish. I was far from being accomplished and that I could not cook or sew or bake but our flat was always very clean because that was the only real chore I knew how and could do. I had a lot to learn and I did, but not without making many amazing mistakes on the way. For example: The soup would burn, boiled egg would run as though uncooked and Spaghetti Bolognaise would turn into a great big cake! (By the way the novel was not "our" love story but a sad tale that we did not peruse the whole book, I don't actually remember what the story was about).

Meanwhile Brian was more of an old soul even though he was only five years older than me. We continued on the roller coaster of life, sometimes it was slow and monotonous, other times it was speeding so fast we were light-headed and almost fell flat. But we survived hanging on to each other, and I still strongly believed that I had a guardian angel who watched over me and perhaps even two or three at times. Oh boy! How I needed them! While Brian was already a master in his own knowledge and was happy to stay put. I was still developing and changing in my perception, my desire, understanding and the self-knowledge in which I sometimes earned my husband's admiration while other times annoyed the hell out of him.

"... Your heart knows in silence the secrets of days and nights. But your ears thirst for the sound of your heart's knowledge. You would know in words that you have always known in thought. You would touch with your fingers the naked body of your dreams..."

Our ten years travelling to foreign soil on diplomatic mission opened our eyes to a lot more knowledge in both good and bad. Brian was doing his job to the utmost best as he had always done knowing I was there for him. As I needed him to be by my side in the beginning, it was his turn to need me. So I too was working hard helping my husband succeed in doing his job. Although diplomatic life looked glamorous there was much emptiness hidden underneath. That was my perception and I could not speak for Brian. He had a job to do and he took his assignment seriously and did not have time to look for any other fulfilment.

1974 Indonesia was ruled under President Suharto for the last eight years - the "Smiling General". Apparently, according to 'Transparency International', he was the most corrupt leader in modern history. Though we all guessed as much no one uttered a word, we talked not of politic in Jakarta let alone criticised the leader of the country, I was only a woman and a wife, my husband did not belong in the political section of the embassy. His job was to promote our country and to communicate with the Press in the host country as well as keeping the Australian based journalists in Jakarta well informed. It was Brian's first posting and he worked hard to deliver. Beside the drama of the end of VN war, the saddest and most disturbing time I remembered was in 1975 when five young Australian journalists were killed in the town of Balibo, East Timor. Brian had to do his job with a heavy heart and I felt for him though he did not discuss it with me in any particular detail, I understood his feelings, coming from being a war correspondent himself not so long ago when he was at the same age of those young men.

Despite what-ever happened, the social circle of the diplomatic corps went on as normal, the dinners, the cocktail parties, the small talks and mingling continued as though we were in a separate world. The husbands talked of politic or whatever while the wives gossiped – who did what, who said what? And who slept with whom? The sort of being sociable with not much intellectual stimulation and conversation, I did not even drink yet I always found myself suffering from terrible headaches returning home from those functions, and you couldn't escape because it happened days after days. I knew many acquaintances but I had no friends and no one I wanted to be friends with. As much as I tried to belong, there was an unknown emptiness. At the time, in Jakarta there was not much for a foreign woman to do on her own, I could not travel anywhere alone without a chauffeur, I could not just walk out of the house and go wandering, it was unheard of.

The heavy social life style in the diplomatic corps did not impress me. I took a trip to Singapore and came back with books, brushes, canvasses, and a dozen tubes of oil colours. I took up painting! I shut myself in the room and instructed the houseboy that I would not receive anyone's calling. I regretted all the women groups' invitations then I painted and painted, canvas after canvas. My first viewers were our servants, they all wanted to have one each. I gave all to them with much pleasure.

At one of the social functions I met an Indonesian artist, he Invited me to attend his exhibition and through him I met many other artists, I purchased a small painting from one of them in which I found much inspiration to keep on painting. Later I invited Mr Sambodja to our house, as he expressed his desire to sketch my portrait. He was also kind enough to give me some basic instructions on the practical side and constructive criticism on my work that helped me enormously. After a few sittings, he gave me one of his sketches. I never knew what he did with the rest. We did not keep in touch.

I managed to produce some decent pieces of artwork, which I put in an exhibition together with other amateur artists just like me and sold a couple of landscapes that made me a very happy artist! Painting became my escape from the onslaught of a heavy-duty social life of Jakarta embassies. Brian couldn't, it was part of his job.

Our time in the US was less hectic in the expected duties on social functions. I guess being in a city that was much larger and where English was the speaking language made our lives much easier. The families of the diplomats had more freedom to move around and were exposed to more alternative interests to fill their days rather than depending just on the diplomatic circle. I joined a local quilting group as well as a painting workshop to occupy my times of the day when my son was at school and my daughter was at day care. Life was good but Brian had to travel more and often he had to be away from home for a whole week at times. His area covered the American East coast to the mid-west plus Alaska, which was quite an extensive stretch. Later, while in San Francisco, he was responsible for an area just as extensive, from California to Texas and from Washington State to Colorado.

We moved into a large house in Bethesda, MD. The day when the removalist van arrived with all our goods was a particularly hot August day. Brian was away interstate on one of his many trips. After the workmen all left, I put myself to work, hoping to get the whole house in order for when Brian returned the next day. He would be pleased to find the place in good shape. It was such a humid day. The children were running around happy to see all the toys that they had not seen for a while. I started to strip as I moved from room to room. The last things I had on were just a pair of undies and an old T/shirt. The doorbell rang, and forgetting about my attire, I went to answer. It was a lady asking me if she could speak to the lady of the house? I told her: *"I am sorry, there's no other lady here."* Then I realised I wasn't dressed at all like a lady. It was my next-door neighbour who I had yet to meet, her name was Mary. She apologised for not knowing I was the lady of the house: *"You look so young!"* she added very tactfully. We became very good friends since and often had a good laugh about it, unfortunately Mary died from an illness quite a long time ago.

In the US, the reign of President Carter was also an interesting time politically. It was not so long after Nixon's resignation; Nixon was the only president that resigned from office, and of course the Watergate scandal, which rocked the whole world. I thought President Carter was a compassionate man and I liked him. He took office in an era of difficult economic climate with so many high expectations that he could not meet. I remembered so clearly the agony and the frustration of the country regarding the Iran hostage crisis for over a year between 1979 -1981. It was a diplomatic standoff between Iran and the US that somehow strengthened the prestige of Ayatollah Khomeini and his political power. But miraculously, within minutes of Reagan's sworn into office, the hostages were free! And so the Iran-Iraq war began. The drama continued ever since... and still because we humans never learn.

The scariest thing happened about six months after we settled down in our home in Maryland. Brian was away in Alaska on one of his trips, a friend and I went to see a film called "The China Syndrome" it was released only about two weeks before. We returned home to learn from the television news that the nuclear accident on Three Mile Island in Dauphin County, Pennsylvania happened on that same day. It was so surreal, quite bizarre really. In one of the scenes the voice of a physicist said: "An area of the size of Pennsylvania would render uninhabitable!" The movie was totally fictional yet the accident of Three Mile Island and the partial meltdown occurred on that day was so significant! I have never forgotten how scare I was.

Westpath Tce, Bethesda

I wished then Brian did not have to travel so much though I knew well it was his job and my job was to support him. Our children were growing into an interesting age and all our attention concentrated on them. The times I loved most, when we were on our little holidays together, just the four of us, when I had my husband and my children all to myself. Holidays never lasted long. The children and I otherwise enjoyed our time discovering and learning the marvel of everyday life in America. When Brian and I were together, our lovemaking was strong and passionate and so were the fierce arguments. Some we solved, and some we resolved to leave till another day. I was still on my learning curve and desperately looking for another self in me, at times it was very confusing yet I had no one to confide in, I drifted in and out between illusion and reality and that went on for a long time. Brian was too busy to notice the change in me, or perhaps he just did not want to know. In restlessness I was searching for the meaning of life, perhaps the quest for infinite understanding and ultimate values. My lack of insight questioned if there were such things.

"... Reason and passion are the rudder and the sails of your seafaring soul. If either your sails or your rudder broken, you can but toss and drift, or else be held at standstill in mid-seas..."

I loved my husband then as I had always loved him. The wheel of life moved on so fast that we did not have time to stop and think, so back on the wheel we moved along. Neither of us could see what lay ahead on the road we yet to travel. Our journey began at different times and different places. Our paths have crossed each other until one day we met to share love and hope. We were about to embark on another journey in which we knew not how it would end.

"... For everything and in every season there is a time... A time for fear and a time for hope..."

From painting oil on canvas I changed to pastel on paper.

"Canberra Lake" Pastel

3

Till the End

*"In one drop of water are found all the secrets of all
the oceans; in one aspect of you are found all the
aspects of existence."*

Kahlil Gibran

"I am irritated *by my own writing. I am like a violinist whose ear is true, but whose fingers refuse to reproduce precisely the sound he hears within.*"

Gustave Flaubert

I am not sure if I write this story to re-live it or to forget. My story is perhaps insignificant to many people, including my children and grandchildren for whom I would like to tell snippets of my life to, I dared say these snippets are also a small part of their story. My husband was very much an accomplished writer and it would have been easy for him to have had done so. Instead, he had insisted that I should be the writer. "*Not in a million years!*" I used to say. Since he left this world for the unknown journey, I have been struggling to write and wished I had listened to my husband when he was alive thus he could have helped me with my writing. Although I could speak three languages, they are all my "seconds". I am not fluent in any of them.

Lately, I am glad to say writing through reading and learning has also been a way that I found myself somehow connecting with Brian's spirit, as though I could communicate with him and I do so want to make him proud of me. I have never claimed to be a professional on anything and especially writing. Painting from the heart was not so difficult when one let the imagination run wild. Writing for me was and still is definitely a thousand times more difficult but I am grateful to have my daughter's support. She had taken up writing at a very young age as her dad did and had in her own way followed her dad's direction. I would not know how I could cope with these last difficult years without the help and support of my daughter.

Seattle 2015

Soon after my thirtieth birthday, I flew from where I was living in Jakarta to Singapore, heavily pregnant, awaiting the birth of my child. According to the medical experts at the time, Singapore hospitals were more advanced and better equipped in case of emergency. So we, diplomat wives were sent off to Singapore to give birth, and yet if you didn't belong to the Diplomatic Corps have the proper diplomatic passport you would be refused an entry visa. It was the immigration law in Singapore at the time. Lee Kuan Yew did not want his little country bombarded by foreigners born in Singapore and claiming citizenship.

My daughter was born at Glen Eagle Hospital. It was one of the best hospitals in the country. On a typical humid Monday afternoon in Singapore, moments after the birth I was totally exhausted, but when I heard one of the nurses say: "Mrs Peck you have a daughter!" I was so happy I thought and felt as though I was floating on top of the clouds. I told Brian some time later that it was the happiest moment ever in my life! Brian said: "*And I thought I was the happiest moment in your life.*" My reply was: "*Well, I made you think that way my darling.*" He smiled and said: "*You could have fooled me, but I don't mind being second.*"

A day later, my baby daughter and I were settled in our room to rest quietly. A Chinese nurse came in to check on us, she whispered anxiously with a concerned look in her eyes: "*Oh, Mrs Peck, your baby looks so European! She doesn't look any Chinese at all.*" In my thoughts: "I bloody well hope not!" I also thought to myself: This nosy little nurse was definitely a gossipmonger in the staff room (General Hospital or Days of our lives???) She thought I was Chinese just by the look of me, and based on my last name "Peck" which filled up the White Page telephone book in Singapore among other names such as Pak and Pek, which are also very popular last names in the country.

Almost thirty more years later, my granddaughter was born in Sydney and her mother said to me: "*Mum, I feel so fulfilled now!*" I was so happy I could cry. My daughter is now a wife and a nurturing mother to her two beautiful children.

Singapore 1977 and Sydney 2005

In the middle of 1998, we were living in Canberra. Both our children had grown up by then and already left home a couple of years earlier. They were living in Sydney pursuing their study and career. Brian took a month holiday leave from his work in Canberra, he went to work in Melbourne to help his old boss write a strategy for her newfound organisation, the sort of work he enjoyed. At that time his work in Canberra was becoming somewhat tedious under a new director who had no idea how to be a director. He also wanted to earn some extra money so we could pay someone to paint our house and fix up around the garden as the whole place had been a little neglected over the past few years. I really enjoyed the opportunity to re-decorate our home, and make it into a new "nest" for us while Brian was in Melbourne. We missed each other during the long month. I took a weekend off flying down to Melbourne to be with Brian. We were so much in love then as though

71

we were in our early years of wedded bliss. At the end of the month, Brian came back to Canberra. He was pleased finding the house and the garden nicely improved after a light transformation. He said:

"It's beautiful darling, what a marvellous job you've done! What do you think about us living in Melbourne?"

"WHAT...? NO!" Said I, horrified!

Within a month Brian was back in Melbourne starting his new job while I was packing in Canberra, putting the house on rental market and ready to move to Melbourne. It was the best move we've made though not without the initial hesitation or resisting on my part. The bitter, sad memory that lasted for almost ten years, which Brian and I have had to go through in order to re-find each other, once again flooded my thoughts. Brian was completely optimistic about it and I could hear his voice:

"Darling, we will try it just for a year and if you absolutely hate it, we'll move back to Canberra. We are different now, we have grown and have learned our lesson..."

I looked into his eyes as though I was searching or pleading for some reassurances, I could feel my eyes sting with unshed tears. We did not take our eyes off each other and slowly he gathered me in his arms kissing my tears before they ran down my cheeks...

"South coast" Pastel

The painful memory happened twelves years earlier (1985). A year after our return home from the US we had just moved into our then new house in Canberra and finally had our belongings coming out from being kept for six years in storage. Within a couple of months, Head Office told Brian that his next post would be in London when it became available in a few months. We, including the children were happy with the news and looked forward to our new post, another adventure! Brian and I agreed that it would be our last posting while the children were still in the early years of schooling. We realised it was then hard enough for our children to settle at school in Canberra after growing up in America. They were at the age when they had become attached to places, friends and life in general. We became more and more conscious that we had the welfare of our children to consider.

The Universe seemed to have another idea for us because a few weeks later, Labour Prime Minister Bob Hawke undertook a huge reshuffle in his cabinet, which caused many changes in all department heads. The new secretary of Brian's department decided to send his chief executive officer to London in order to get him out of sight and replaced him with a preferred new person. There went our London post! Brian resigned, not because he lost London, but because he was not at all happy at the desk job and did not want to waste each day being unhappy. Soon after, he joined a PR company and we all moved to Melbourne instead. That was the year of my unhappiest time with Brian...

We rented a nice big house in Burwood a suburb in Camberwell on the outskirts of Melbourne. It was a strange decision for me to make. In this suburb, beside many big houses and gardens on big wide leafy streets, it was a place devoid of any character. Our children struggled settle into new schools yet again, making new friends, and getting used to the new way of living. Brian devoted his time proving himself in the new workplace environment, new bosses and new colleagues. My job was to keep my family happy. I had no time or inspiration for much else, nor any desire for painting or creating anything new. Time seemed to stand still as though I was waiting for something to happen, something to appear through the mist of a mundane existence but I knew not what. Every day passed by you dreamt without sleeping and longing for night. Then when night came, you slept without dreaming only to wake for another of the same.

I did not crave for any passion or rapture as the women in the 1800s romantic novels. Even sex did not have the power to restore the missing bits in our relationship. Though I knew the difference between love and infatuation, and though my love for my husband was strong and deep, it did not stop me from letting my emotion run wild with illusion. This started to happen during the years living in the US when I started to compare my husband with other men. My lack of wisdom and insight saw me chasing certain false beliefs, fuelled by external influences, and not recognising the change within me – either good or bad. Or perhaps I was still too immature in my thinking to have had enough confidence and strength to acknowledge the truth of the situation, be it a real desire or a fantasy. In a total confused state of mind, which I could not understand clearly myself let alone be brave enough to confide in anyone, the only person I trusted was my husband but even then I still could not talk with him. At times I tried but he appeared not to want to listen. Perhaps he had guessed whatever in his mind and thought if we did not mention "it", in time "it" would go away. I too thought the same at one stage, but it did not go away. The irritation, the awkwardness and the unsatisfactory feelings started to become more apparent between us. I questioned love?

"Love is perhaps a mere imposture of our boredom and our great hopes. It may have risen from an artificial passion built from scratch."

Jean d'Ormesson

That year in Melbourne Brian and I drifted apart. I cried a lot mostly out of frustration. I went looking for outside interests and tempted to further study in art and painting but my heart was disillusioned, nothing to learn and nothing to feel. Once there was nourishment in our trouble-free communication. Then, it seemed to be almost impossible even at the best of times when Brian was sober and I was in my good mood. We talked less and less and only in fragments and so unconnected yet we continued to live on in a habitual daily life, one habit among others like a dessert that one looked forward to, after the monotony of dinner. The saddest thing was that our children sensed something was wrong and it pained me as much as it did Brian. One day, when we did talk and nothing positive came out of it, we decided on a trial separation. The children and I moved back to our house in Canberra, while Brian stayed in Melbourne continuing with his work. The year that followed was full of longing and sadness, I thought of Brian days and nights even though I lead a busy life with a part-time job and looking after the children – their everyday living and their emotional states of mind, as they too missed Brian.

Perhaps the Universe had planned it that way, and that we needed an awakening. During the months of living separately, although I was sad and unhappy, it was a different sort of unhappiness. In my solitude, I found the time and the space that I needed to look within, to question the reason and the passion that went through my life since that day when this handsome young reporter who helped me carry my bags... He had occupied a large chunk in my heart. The flame was still burning bright. I realised then that I always loved him and nothing could influence me otherwise. I stuck to my mundane job and caring for my children, I made some friends and enjoyed a little bit of a social life but I went no further and I looked no where else. I only wanted my husband back to me, to a fresh start. Any illusion that had been hanging over my head slowly waned and in the end there was no one, no matter how dashing he might have been to my eyes that could compare to my husband's love and devotion. That strong belief stayed with me since, despite how many temptations or hard times I encountered for another few more years yet to come, before Brian and I truly found each other again. Thus I could only speak for myself; I did not know what was in Brian's thoughts during those years. Not until when we were reunited that he confided in me: "*... I was so terrified that if I should lose you, it would be so intolerable. I don't know how I could cope without you in my life. I felt so sick in my gut mentally and to the point of almost physically... Oh darling how I love you!*"

After the first year of separation, Brian returned to live with us in Canberra. He opened a branch for the same PR Company in Melbourne. He also worked in Sydney and travelled between the three cities regularly. I changed to working full time and from time to time I too had my trips away from home. Brian and I were still in the middle of searching for answers, for solutions, for reason and passion as we re-learned our way to better communication. The children went through higher school and college without too many dramas. We spent some times separately and at times together, with many more ups and downs until well into 1997. When the magic returned and my husband and I were once again re-united as though we came together from across the ocean of our beginning. I did not forget to thank my guardian angels (the number must have increased to half a dozen by then) I imagined they must have had an enormous amount of patience helping me. Since then Brian and I hung on to each other with much more understanding and appreciation between us. I guess even with love so strong, each of us needs the time and the place to grow into maturity, it doesn't matter how old we were. I was then one and fifty and I realised that almost my whole forties were but a learning curve through many trials and errors. I was as always – a slow learner.

Surrey Road, South Yarra

Our second time moving to Melbourne went smoothly. Brian laughed when I told him that we would stay well clear of Camberwell and said he had no intention to return to that suburb, though we were sure many people who lived there were happy. We rented a little house in South Yarra, a trendy and busy suburb closed to the city by train. Our little house was cute and cosy, just right for the two of us. The lift van arrived, and as it happened in Winter I did not need to work in the heat setting up the house as in Washington. Brian had to be in the office for some important meetings so again I was happy working alone putting things into orders. In the evening when Brian arrived home, he saw a hundred and fifty boxes were unpacked, and the house was beautifully arranged. When I greeted him, he was holding a huge bouquet at the door with a big smile on his face. We hugged and I felt so safe and secure, we both felt like we were the newlyweds again, even though more than twenty-five years had past since. Brian whispered in my ear: *"It is so nice coming home, my darling..."*

From painting in pastel, I plucked up the courage to step into watercolour. It was not as easy as walking into a "puddle" of my childhood but I had no fear or felt any reproach, I sought no control but to let the gentle flow of water taking me to another creative scenario that was full of love, rapture and delight.

"Watercolour is a swim in the metaphysics of life... a mirror of one's own character. Let it be unpredictable and colourful."

"On the bay" Watercolour

We only meant to stay in Melbourne for one year and I am still here nineteen years later. The longest time I lived in any city on earth. Most of the time we were happy, we still had little tiffs and arguments now and then but they were all resolved and we always kissed and made up before going to sleep. Brian never stopped working, he could have had retired many years ago but he was needed for his talent and he felt good to be needed, also he never could say "no". I was proud of him and all the things he chose to do. We also had many good voyages travelling overseas for holidays, which took me a few years to convince him to do, and once he did and had a taste of it he looked forward to new trip every year.

I remembered when living in Jakarta, I was supposed to meet him at the office early in the evening so we could attend a work function. I arrived early. Brian showed me a telex from head office in Canberra inviting staff to put in proposals for up coming postings, one was in Paris. I was delighted and urging him to put in for it. He disdainfully told me that he considered it was the last place on earth he would want to be and there was no way he would apply for it. I insisted "Paris! Darling, Paris!" Hoping to change his mind. He casually tossed the piece of paper in the wastebasket. I was so mad I walked out of the office and asked the chauffeur to take me home before returning for Brian later. He thought that was quite an amusing scene and teased me about it for a long time afterwards.

In 2009 when we had the opportunity to spend a week in Paris, Brian agreed to do it just to please me for it was his first visit ever to this most romantic city. He fell in love with the place! The first evening after we arrived at our rented apartment in Quartier Latin, we walked around the area and found a local café for a quick dinner. Rain started to fall, as we were about to walk back, Brian pulled out a little folded umbrella from his pocket that was old and damaged attempting to shield us from the rain. I only had a few sips of wine with my dinner but I was in such high spirits, merely because I was so happy to be in Paris and with my husband! I took the umbrella off him and tossed it in the bin by the footpath. The shock on his face sent my laughter high and loud and before he could utter a word I said earnestly in excitement: *"Darling, we are in Paris, we don't need that stupid umbrella, we just walk in the rain, come on let's go!"* When he could speak: *"you silly little bugger, we'll get soaked!"* Like a couple of over-excited kids, we skipped and danced, we both stepped into so many puddles together sending them plashing. The raindrops caught the streetlight reflection that sparkled like stars. We sang and laughed all the way home and yes we did get totally soaked from head to toe. So soaked that we had problems pulling off our wet clothes back at the apartment but with laughter still.

Later, Brian told me he had had the best time from that first evening and that he would not mind visiting Paris again but we did not have another chance to be back before he fell ill.

I am not sure if I ever want to see Paris again, I have been to Paris half a dozen times before, but that last trip was the happiest time of all. How could I laugh and dance again without Brian.

The years living in Melbourne and my watercolour painting brought me more joy than I've ever imagined. I produced works that sold in several galleries across Melbourne and interstate as well as overseas, just by words of mouth from satisfied customers. A dozen or so gentlewomen wanted to have lessons with me so our little house became painting classes in the kitchen, on the dining table twice a week. Brian was my "patron saint" and he supported my endeavour and me totally. He was the most kind and generous husband any woman would wish for. Though I did not wish to gloat, I was quite certain there were a few jealous females out there who did not like me at all.

"In a forest" Watercolour

One woman who I knew only superficially asked me how did Brian and I meet. When briefly I told her the story that happened at Singapore airport. She looked at me and said in the most patronizing manner: "*You were very lucky to have met Brian"*. I agreed with her totally and my reply was: *"He was damn lucky to have met me too."* When I later told Brian, he was quite amused: *"Oh darling, she must have thought I plucked you from the rice-paddy in Vietnam!"* That made me laugh too and we both agreed to wonder which 'bourgeoisie' of the peasant stock she came from.

"I have no enemy; I have some good friends and not so good a friend. Those who don't like me don't deserve to be anywhere near my thoughts, they do not exist."

"South Yarra" Watercolour

We loved living in South Yarra and we never went anywhere near that "strange" suburb again. We had a wonderful time exploring the country around the state of Victoria as well as other suburbs in Melbourne. But if Brian had plenty of money he would have had moved back to Sydney as quick as a flash, Sydney had always been his most favourite city in the world. Even as I began to enjoy living in Melbourne more and more, I told Brian I would be happy wherever we went as long as we were together. I remember saying something like that to my daughter when she was at the tender age of five and half. Soon after we came back from America, my little daughter burst into tears one day. When asked why, she said: *"I am homesick!"* She was missing our place in San Francisco, her kindergarten class, her little friends and the way of life she knew all her life thus far. My poor darling, I kissed her teary face and hugged her close to my chest: *"Darling, home is where we are, where ever the four of us are."* She never cried again on that subject. During the year of my separation from Brian, I was so miserable remembering what I told my daughter and I felt totally devastated, perhaps that helped me to think a thousand thoughts in looking to find a way to mend my children's pain. Both our children have now made their home within their own "foursome" in different cities of far-away lands for many years. Brian and I missed them but we preferred to think of our children and grandchildren with happy thoughts and not miss them with misery. We never dreamt of making any demands on our children though they'd always have our unconditional love.

As time moved on and Brian's health deteriorated, one tranquil afternoon just for a gentle diversity I took out Brian's old scrapbook and we looked through it together on the dining table. A feeling though not declared as if we both wanted to re-capture his youth (and mine). We read all the little quotes and poems he collected but forgot over the years. There were various letters to the newspapers, old photographs, then we came to a page that was not in his handwriting – a little prose written by someone whom I gathered must have once been in love with Brian. I knew it was before my time but I teased him all the same to see a smile and a blush on his pale face. *"Ah ha! That magenta is a dead give-a-way darling!"* said I. With a quiet smile, he replied softly: *"It was long before your time my darling, you are my only true love."* I hugged his frail body gently and kissed his forehead most tenderly, he could not see the tears in my eyes. I wanted time to stand still.

Soon after Brian died, I had no idea how she knew but another woman wrote to me, her name: "Jenny" from Florida, USA – a brief message: *"I worked with Brian many years ago and I have been crying buckets here in Florida, he was the love of my life!"* Someone asked me: *"How do you feel Thai?"* My reply: *"I am glad there is someone else crying buckets too and not just me!"*

Looking through the old scrapbook Brian and I also found his old business cards. The address: 23 "Hàn Thuyên" Saigon.

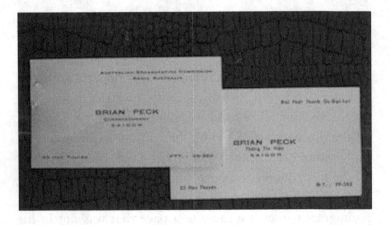

The address caught my eyes and my memory raced back to Saigon days when Brian rented a flat above a hairdressing salon. 1968 in Saigon around the city area or anywhere near the centre, accommodation was hard to find unless you were prepared to rent a hotel room at The Continental Palace Hotel as some journalists and cameramen did. Even then, sometimes they had to share one room and work out when one was on the field so the other could use the room, very complicated. Brian decided to venture outside, not so far from the centre of the city and chose to live on a pretty and leafy street between the Saigon Cathedral and the Presidential Palace. From one end of the long wide avenue lined with green park on each side stood an imposing palace, past the cathedral you'll come to the strong iron gate of the US embassy... and a little further down to the other end of the long avenue stood the Saigon zoo.

To visit Brian in his apartment I had to walk past the salon under the scrutiny eyes of all the female workers as well as the customers. It was the most uncomfortable feeling knowing that gossip was going to fly probably across town and get to my mother's ears. Yet when Brian walked by, the women young and old were just all over him offering him all sorts of services: "Mr Peck, you want hair cut? Manicure...? Brian told me he did not care to have a haircut in the salon. He waited until his monthly trip to Singapore and have it done by a barber over there instead. I certainly would not have had anything to do with the salon, his landlady sometimes greeted me and I politely said hello back but I had never wanted to converse with her what so ever.

At the landing of the staircase, his apartment looked comfortable enough for a bachelor. The strangest thing was that the room had no door. Just as well, ABC cameraman Allan Lee, who was working with Brian and whom we knew well, occupied the only other room across the landing. And yes, Allan's room had a proper door and he was so nice telling me that he would have swapped rooms with Brian but he had all his precious cameras and equipment that needed to be kept in a secured place.

Han Thuyen Street was one of the best addresses in the city, across from the residential side. It looked to an avenue of trees uninterrupted as I remembered. It was like a park full of beautiful ancient trees and the shade provided a lovely cool air when you walked under, a place to escape from the heat in the humid climate. As a kid I often played with my siblings and various cousins under those big trees, where there were so many puddles for me to jump into. I never imagined then just across that quiet little street, it was written in the stars that would one day be the place where my future husband would be living for 19 months.

As I am writing 'my story' it is coming up to the second anniversary of my husband's death. I have never experienced such a loss in my life. I have never missed anyone or anything as I am missing Brian. I am not just a widow but also an orphan for without Brian, I feel as though I am all alone in the world. I am grateful to have had the last twenty years of Brian's life in which we shared our love so fully and unselfishly. We were indeed lucky! To have had survived all obstacles that was thrown our way till the end.

In November 2014 my husband went on a working trip to London for ten days. I was recovering from a major surgery and could not accompany him. It was his last trip ever and it was perhaps the trip that caused his illness to worsen, he never could recover from the exhaustion of the long journey, and death was fast approaching within four months.

Our communication between England and Australia during the time being apart:

> *Melbourne office 17/11/2014*
> *"This is where I am staying Darling – FYI:*
> *An Italian heart beats in the heart of London.*
> *The Baglioni Hotel London is situated in the heart of London, the cosmopolitan city par excellence, opposite Hyde Park with an enchanting view of Kensington Gardens and Palace. The hotel is situated a short distance from historic and cultural places of interest and the shops and watering holes that animate the city's nightlife; the Royal Albert Hall, Harrods and Knightsbridge are nearby. The entirely Italian hospitality and luxury services offered such as the spa, fitness center, chauffeur-driven car and personal butler would make your stay in London truly unforgettable."*
> *Not that I will get a chance to enjoy it all – but I will try.*
> *Bp*

21/11/2014
I am at Dubai airport darling. Slept
ok. No problems anywhere.
How are you? Did you try driving and was it ok? How
are you feeling? Not much fun without you. Didn't
bother to talk to my next-door neighbour – we both
went to sleep anyway. Many of the passengers were
young men and women business professionals,
Working on their laptops while watching videos with
headphones on. I don't know how they do it.
Lots of love.
b...

Cambridge 22/11/2014
I loved your cheerful report on your Friday walkabout.
I hope you are doing ok and not over-doing it.
My 'un-eventual' trip took a different turn when the counter
clerk at Dubai directed me to the wrong gate and I missed
the plane. Emirates profusely apologised and admitted it was
there fault. They finally got me on another flight but in all I
spent a day at the airport. When we got onto the plane and
settled in, we were told the plane was faulty and we had to
get on another plane, which left two hours later. The one good
thing is that Emirates honoured the car trip to Cambridge
but it was after midnight when I climbed into bed.
This morning I bought an excellent overcoat.
We have been hanging out at home today with Ferne
playing with the other kids. We are going out for an early
dinner tonight. Weather is overcast and cool - not too bad.
You have been in our thoughts all day, and I am missing you.
Lots of love, B...

My reply: From Chelsea/Melbourne:

I am glad you bought yourself a good coat. But the second leg of the journey did not turn out as well as I had hoped for you. I hope you recovered okay after all the hassles.

I went to bed at my normal time last night (10 PM) only to be woken up soon after midnight with loud argument noises from a group of party-goers on the street. They were young men and women in their mid-twenty from a birthday party around the corner at the end of Golden Ave. I went to the window to watch the whole drama unfold. :) Their voices were so loud and clear standing at the front of the house across the street, I think everyone could hear them; waking up all the children and the dogs.

Today (Sun) I am going for a little walk on the sand this morning for my exercise. No, I am not overdoing it. I think I know my limit. Love you. TP

From Cambridge
I hope you enjoyed your walk darling.
They were not party-goers but selfish A-holes.
Shame somebody didn't call the cops.
We stayed in doors all Afternoon, mostly being entertained by Ferne. Then it was dinner at a family restaurant. Everybody ate very well and were well behaved and had fun. Today we planned to go to the park but I see that it is raining, maybe I will suggest a swim in the hotel pool. Everybody has been asking after you and I have told them how resilient you are. So stay strong. Love you darling. bp

From Chelsea:

How are you? Darling, you should be asleep at this time!!!

I enjoyed my little walk on the sand this morning, bought a croissant at the French deli and had it with my coffee at home. I feel stronger everyday.

Adam called today and Katherine also. Teresa called everyday. They all worried that I am lonely, but I feel good being by myself just for this week, to daydream and communicate with myself, very relaxing!

Are you okay?
♥

From London
Yes darling, I am fine thank you.
I have had poor Internet connections and now my time is fully occupied but everything is going well. I am balancing handling Melbourne requests with our London work.
I am so glad everybody is providing you with support.
I hope that you are feeling better every day.
I have had to delay my departure by one day, and will now arrive in Melbourne at 9:35pm on Saturday.
I will write more tonight.
Love, bp

From London 26/11/2014
I hope that you are continuing to improve my darling. How have you been sleeping, and is the pain and discomfort reducing?

After a wet Sunday, Monday dawned bright, clear and frosty.
The train ride was early enough to see the fields covered in a
light frost and mist rising from the ground as the sun began
to 'warm' – it was so beautiful that I thought of you and your
camera, and wondered if I could capture the scene in words.
Michelle and I spent the rest of the day talking,
talking, and talking. Roughing out plans on pieces
of paper until we were both exhausted.
Today's meeting with Sam and his colleague Niccolas
(who is from Belgium) went well and we covered a lot of
ground but we can see there is much more work to do.
I am hoping that tomorrow will be a lighter day – and
we have another meeting on Thursday, which is why
I have to delay my return by about 24 hours.
I think Michelle is having room service and I have to
go out to find some dinner. This is a lovely hotel, with
over the top service and food but I need a break.
Thank goodness for my coat. Love,
b...

From Chelsea:

I hope you have a good dinner and a good walk and sleep well
tonight.

I am fine and pain is slowly going away. I don't take the
panadol anymore, just only when needed and only one instead
of two. Sleeping is okay too, one night is better than the other,
doesn't really matter, I still have enough sleep.

Thai Peck

Sound as though you are flat out with your brain, take a bit of time off to smell the rose, if there is any? Hope the next couple of days are easier for you.

Did you re-book the Qantas car to pick you up both ends?

Take care,
Love, Thai

> *From London*
> *Thank you darling.*
> *I had a pleasant walk – cool but not wet – to a busy and crowded little restaurant where I had a bowl of pumpkin soup and a glass of merlot.*
> *It was fun looking and listening to everybody and watching people and traffic out of the window. I passed an ice-skating rink, which was very crowded but looked fun.*
> *I hope you have a good day.*
> *bp*

> *28/11/2014*
> *I hope everything is ok with you darling. No roses to smell but we did take your advice: on Wednesday afternoon we grabbed an hour or so to look at an exhibition of Rembrandt's later works at the national gallery.*
>
> *Yesterday I took Michelle to our favourite coffee shop at St Pancreas station for a light lunch, and to look and listen to travellers. We had been meeting nearby and I was able to show her the hotel and the big statue. I had a green juice and wrote down the recipe for you, which includes Brussels sprouts. I am sorry that I have been so poor in*

emailing you but each evening I have gone to bed very early, usually not bothering about dinner. Not only do I have no appetite but I don't even fancy a drink. Very little traffic to the airport this morning, which means I arrived early but this was good because it was easy to negotiate security and take a gentle walk to the business lounge. Michelle thanked me for coming and said I had made useful contributions. But of course I can't wait to get back to you.

Love,

Your husband

From Chelsea:

Everything is fine here. I am glad you had a bit of time out from the serious stuff. You must be so tired not to bother about dinner. I hope you are okay and that you can have good sleep on the way back. I am looking forward to your return.

I love you,

TP

I did not know then, it would be our last email communication, yet I wondered what could I have done if I knew...

Tasmania 2007

Warrnambool 2012

8/04/2015
Last email from Brian: A farewell?

Hi folks

We went to the oncologist, Dr Andrew Hayden, today and looked at the last scan, and while it is a few weeks old it shows that the cancers have not spread, which is good news.

Andrew told us that he did not believe more chemo treatment would help, if anything it could have an adverse effect on the cancers. For this reason I have decided not to subject myself to more treatment but rather accept the inevitable rather than the unknown side effects of chemo. My 'health professionals' do not know how long the inevitable will be. They speak only in averages – some people live longer than others.

I believe that if I keep on working (within reason), fed by Thai's excellent meals, some of which are laced with Aloe Vera and keep positive I will be one who lives longer.

The biggest downside continues to be shortage of breath, which severely limits walking so Thai and I will look for a light, folding wheel chair so I can get around. Talking can be a problem also.

Medication that I am taking is keeping pain at bay – in fact I have only had a few painful episodes. I take the medicine even before I can feel the pain coming on, and this helps with conversation.

In the meantime I will invite one or two people to pop in and see me, without kids because I don't have the energy to entertain them.

We really appreciate the family visits and looking forward to Sam's arrival next weekend.

I have asked Thai to forward this email to family and friends whose addresses I do not have.

Brian

Brian died 10 April 2015

"... Remember me when I am gone away... far away.

...When you can no more hold me by the hand...

Remember me when no more day by day...

And if you should forget me for a while...

Better by far you should forget and smile...

Than that you should remember and be sad"

Christina Rossetti

"Blue bench" Watercolour

Alone I sit now that you've gone away

I miss you more and more each day

No more can I kiss your soft tender lips

No hands to hold or touch each finger tips..."

Robert Harrison

The End

"Summer creek" Watercolour

Epilogue

A lovely summer evening and my dinner out with a couple of friends was a pleasant occasion as usual – at a local restaurant about twenty minutes walk from my house. The evening twilight was soft and the temperature became less hot and less humid as we were walking back. My friends and I said goodnight at the fork on the road that lead one way to their house, while I carried on the other way towards mine. As I was walking I realised the street seemed long and somehow I was not on the same familiar street to my house yet I did not remember making any turn. The summer evening suddenly turned into night, the street was deserted and the streetlights were somehow never bright enough for my vision. I kept on walking and hoping perhaps at the next intersection I could see clearer. Alas! To my disappointment, it was not my street but one that I did not recognise.

In the distance far away I could see a numbers of bright lights, which I guessed must be a shopping street and perhaps it was where my local shops were, if I get there I would be able to find my way home. Unfortunately when I approached the lit up area, it was not my local shopping strip. I saw a woman busy closing up her shop. I stopped her and asked for the direction to my street. She told me that should not be too difficult – if I kept walking on the little lane by the side of her shop and turned left at the end of the lane, then I would be able to see my local shopping area, which will then lead the way to my street.

I did as she directed, only to find a creek running across the laneway and there was no easy way to cross it let alone be able to turn left. I rushed back to the shop and caught the shop owner before she left and told her about the creek. She looked at me and smiled calmly telling me that I should use my imagination to cross it. *"It's not hard!"* she added and walked away as if to tell me: *"No big deal! Don't be such a wuss!"*

Decided I could not get any more help out of her, I walked back to the creek. As I was walking along the side of the running creek trying to figure out how I should cross it. In the late evening light the creek looked dark and unfriendly but I imagined in the daylight it would be a pretty sight for a watercolour painting, thick with shrubs, wild flowers and tall grass along the bank. Even though it was not such a wide creek it would be impossible for me to jump across for fear I might slip and hurt myself.

As I was searching for a way to cross, I saw one lonely wooden fence on my side of the creek and after judging it, I carefully climbed over the fence then gingerly moving along the edge until where I could see the embankment that was wide and the creek that was narrow enough for me to jump across without too much effort. (As the woman said: *it was not hard!*)

Once safely crossed the embankment on the other side I walked to the end of the laneway. A left turn and sure enough I could see some bright lights in the distance as the shopkeeper said that should be my local shopping area. The night was getting darker without the moonlight and the street became eerier yet the distance to the village seemed to be ever so far. I started to panic, looking around I wondered about my safety. All of a sudden I felt so tired from all the walking knowing it would still be another twenty minutes further after I reached the local village shops. Home was like an illusion.

I could not see anyone on the street yet I felt as though I was followed. Fear came over me and I began to quicken my pace to almost running... My heartbeats were pumping fast. I decided to run even though I could not see clearly far down the road. Faster and faster I ran, so fast that I surprised myself as I knew I have always been a slow walker let alone running, and with my heart's condition I could never run that fast! I looked down at my feet and saw they were on roller skate wheels...

"Should I wake out of a dream or should I continue on my journey?" A journey that would be totally new and unknown, and it seemed as though I could not turn back once I crossed that creek, and to go back I would not have been able to find my way because nothing stayed the same. The secured place of dwelling that kept me happy and safe once was no longer there. My roller skates were the vehicles that would enable me moving from my fear and with the help of one particular guardian angel, to the new journey I shall go forth...

Acknowledgement

Kahlil Gibran (The Prophet) who inspired me with his wisdom and knowledge.

Dorothea Mackellar whose verses drew a perfect picture of this beautiful land, Australia.

Sarah Teasdale whose poem ignited thoughts and feelings that I was not able to describe and in which I was grateful.

Gustave Flaubert, **Jean d'Ormesson**, **Christina Rossetti** whose books and poems I enjoyed reading and growing up with.

Robert Harrison for the last poem, which spoke my sentiment perfectly.

Good friends who read and supported my endeavour through "My Puddles" I thank you from the bottom of my heart.

Readers' comments

Val Sheppard: "I enjoyed your journey through the book immensely and realised how much love and trust you had in Brian (and I guessed the determination in yourself) to venture away from your home country. Your children and grandchildren are fortunate that you could put Brian's and your stories down on paper for them to know and appreciate. The way you have inserted your paintings photos and verses with appropriate meanings to the chapters is very clever."

Hazel Harvey: "Well, I have just read your book for the second time, and loved every minute of it, for your love, emotions and patience. It's just so sad that your adored Brian was taken at a young age, but it is not in our hands. As you appreciate the powers that he gave you a most exciting and unimaginable life in other countries through Brian's job, and you have all the memories to relive, also your adored children and grandchildren. You said your English is not so good, but I think it was great to read, and it was just you; with no fuss about perfection in a language other than your mother tongue."

Arnold Harvey: "I just want to say how much I enjoyed reading your book and your amazing experiences at home and abroad. It's a wonderful tribute to your late husband

Brian as you intended. Wishing you much joy and happiness in the future."

Rosemary Dan: "Well I finally finished your amazing book at 3am!!! I am still in tears. So much passion, so much joy, so much sorrow and so much more all inspiring me in so many ways. You are an artist not only through your painting but also through your writing, your words. You are so eloquent and you took me on an incredible journey. It took me quite a while to read it because I got swept away by so much emotion and then I had to reread every passage through my fascination and by the fact that your writing just drew me in as though I was watching a movie.

Lynne Pocknee: "Thai has lived a big, rich and bold life - one that had taken her far from her birthplace - and much of it accompanied by Brian, the great love of her life. This brave memory, although about loss, reassures that the presence of love can always be kept close."

Linley Wallis: "If I have to describe Thai Peck's "My Puddles" in just two words they would be "love story". Thai's account of her childhood is shadowy, with undertones of unhappiness and dissatisfaction. From her first meeting with Brian there is a complete change of tone and what follows is an account of deep love, personal development, discovery, great hardship and great joy. Her personal journey shines through it all and is deepened and enhanced by her paintings and photographs.

Ralf Boetker: "Thai Peck's fascinating, true story of lifelong love, enhanced with her paintings, photos and poems is inspiring and captivating."

Teresa Hao Nguyen: "My Puddles is a beautiful story in her heartfelt writing, Thai Peck provided a vivid chronology with pictures adding powerful impact to her story."

Helen Sale: "I have enjoyed reading Thai Peck's book "My Puddles". It is an interesting and honest account of her love story, which enriched by her beautiful paintings. My late husband also did his tour of duty in Vietnam around the same time as Brian Peck, he was with the 3rd Battalion, Royal Australian Regiment. We were married for 43 years until his death in 2014. So in some ways our life has had similarities. I wish I had some of her artistic talent."

Xavier Nguyen: "Très bon livre avec une belle mise en page et de magnifiques photos issues de peintures faites par l'auteur et de photos personnelles d'époque. Un récit qui vous fait voyager à travers le monde et qui relate la vie d'une jeune vietnamienne rencontrant l'amour de sa vie sous les bombes."

Brian Peck reported from Saigon

A video Link:

https-//www.youtube.com#2DF79A1

Printed in the United States
By Bookmasters